Series 649
A Ladybird Book

*Throughout this book you will find numbers in brackets after some sentences. The following list of these numbers indicates places in the Bible which you will find interesting to read.*

(1)   Luke 2, v. 7
(2)   Luke 2, vv. 21-22
(3)   Matthew 25, vv. 6-7
(4)   Matthew 3, v. 12
(5)   John 10, v. 7
(6)   Matthew 25, v. 32
(7)   Luke 10, v. 13
(8)   Matthew 3, v. 3
(9)   Luke 10, v. 35
(10)  John 18, v. 1
(11)  Luke 1, v. 9
(12)  Mark 12, vv. 41-42
(13)  Luke 2, v. 46
(14)  Mark 12, vv. 38-39
(15)  Deuteronomy 6, vv. 4-9
(16)  Luke 4, v. 20
(17)  Psalm 19, vv. 9-10
(18)  Acts 22, v. 3
(19)  Luke 23, vv.7-12
(20)  Matthew 2, v. 22
(21)  Matthew 5, v. 41
(22)  Luke 3, v. 2
(23)  Mark 2, vv. 14-15
(24)  Mark 15, v. 34
(25)  John 9, vv. 16, 34
(26)  Acts 9, vv. 1-2

# LIFE
# IN NEW
# TESTAMENT
# TIMES

by RALPH R. GOWER, B.D., DIP. ED.

with illustrations by ERIC WINTER

Ladybird Books Loughborough

## *Palestine—the Coastline and Countryside*

Palestine is a hilly country no larger than Wales. In New Testament times it was important because main trade routes from Europe, Africa and Asia passed through it. Powerful countries surrounding Palestine fought to control it because taxes paid by merchants and travellers were a source of great wealth.

To the west of Palestine is the Mediterranean Sea. The coastline in the south is sandy and without harbours. The Jews did not become good sailors, but instead became farmers and grew crops on the coastal land.

A long row of hills runs parallel to the coastline. In the south, in Judaea, these form a desert, and it was here that Jesus faced His temptations. Further north, in Samaria, they are more fertile, and grapes are grown on hill terraces. There was only one route through the hills —along the broad valley of Esdraelon which was therefore the most fought-over valley of all.

East of the hills is the River Jordan, which begins at Mount Hermon in the north and flows south through the Sea of Galilee. Jesus often visited the hills which surround the Sea of Galilee. Many people lived in the lakeside towns of Bethsaida, Capernaum and Tiberias. Beyond the river, the hills are flatter, and trees, cattle and crops are plentiful, but further east still, the land merges into the Arabian Desert.

*A relief map of Palestine*

0 7214 0223 2

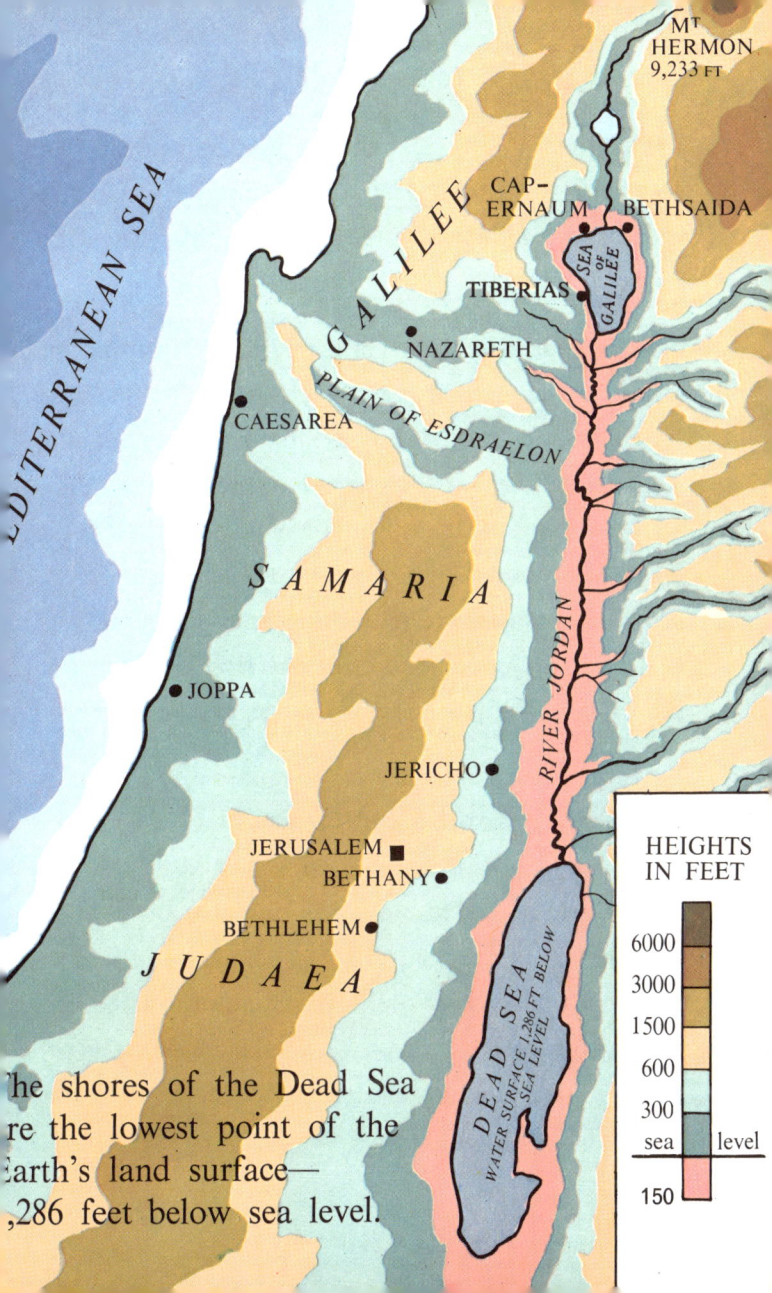

MEDITERRANEAN SEA

Mᵀ HERMON 9,233 FT

GALILEE

CAP-ERNAUM

BETHSAIDA

SEA OF GALILEE

TIBERIAS

NAZARETH

PLAIN OF ESDRAELON

CAESAREA

SAMARIA

RIVER JORDAN

JOPPA

JERICHO

JERUSALEM

BETHANY

BETHLEHEM

J U D A E A

DEAD SEA WATER SURFACE 1,286 FT BELOW SEA LEVEL

The shores of the Dead Sea are the lowest point of the Earth's land surface—1,286 feet below sea level.

HEIGHTS IN FEET

6000
3000
1500
600
300
sea level
150

## The Weather

Palestine is fairly near the equator, so generally the weather is hot and dry. In winter, however, it is much colder in the hills than in the low, sheltered valley of the River Jordan.

In summer it is so hot in the Jordan valley that the water evaporates almost as soon as it reaches the Dead Sea. The water in this lake gets more and more salt until nothing can live in it. This gives it its name. Because it is so salty, things float easily and it is possible to sit in the water without sinking. The heat encourages jungle growth around the river, and sometimes this is so thick that it is only possible to cross the river easily in two places—just below the Sea of Galilee, and near Jericho.

Most of the rain falls in the autumn, and this is important because the soil becomes soft enough for ploughing, and the water cisterns are filled. Autumn rains were called 'former rains' in Bible times. The spring rains (or 'latter rains') encourage the growth of the crops and spring flowers. Soon afterwards the hot, scorching wind blows across the Arabian Desert and the flowers wither and die, except near the coast where the sea mists keep them alive.

*Crops and spring flowers after the rains*

# Homes of the Wealthy and the Poor

The type of house in which people live depends on the local climate and the amount of money they can afford to spend. Because the weather in Palestine is normally hot and dry, in New Testament times the walls of the houses were made of thick stone and whitewashed to keep out the heat. There was no glass in the windows; staircases were built outside and there were open spaces between rooms. A cistern for catching rain-water was essential.

In the homes of the wealthy, rooms were built round a central courtyard, and one courtyard opened into another, very often containing beautiful gardens. In such homes, servants did most of the work, and there was every comfort. The rich sat at tables and on couches; they used beds, chairs and cushions similar to those which we use today. Music, entertainment and high-class cooking were to be found in the homes of the very rich.

The poorer homes were simple dwellings, like up-turned shoe-boxes. Outside was a staircase to the roof, which was made of branches plastered with mud. There was a mud floor inside with a raised platform where the family ate and slept. Animals shared the mud floor.

*Wealthy homes with courtyards*

## Life with a Peasant Family

The Jewish peasant family slept on thin mattresses on a platform at the end of the house. Light was from an oil lamp—Jews never slept without a light. The crowing of a cockerel, or perhaps movement among the animals on the mud floor, would awaken the family and they would rise quickly and take the mattresses outside to air them. Soon breakfast would be ready—goat's milk and dried fruit, or olives and bread.

The men went off to the fields quickly before the sun made it too hot to work. Mother and children went to the village well, each carrying an earthenware jar on their heads. Mother carried a leather bucket on a long rope to get the water. There was time to have a chat with the other women from the village before returning home to sweep the house.

The most important job was the making of bread. Corn kept in a hole in the house wall was sorted to remove dust and poisonous seeds. Mother put some on a hot metal plate over the charcoal fire to make parched corn—like puffed wheat. The rest was ground between two millstones, and after being 'leavened' with some dough left over from the day before, it was baked in a tiny oven.

*Interior view of peasant home*

## *Important Days in the Jewish home*

The arrival of a new baby was a very important occasion, especially if the baby was a boy. Girls were not thought very important in New Testament times. When a baby was born, it was rubbed all over with salt, as people believed this made the skin firm, and then it was wrapped in a tight cloth like a bandage to help it grow straight. This was called 'swaddling' (1). Eight days later a boy was taken to a priest for a service of dedication to God and was given his name (2).

It was the custom for parents to arrange marriages, and weddings took place after a 'betrothal' and before the bride and groom were twenty years old. The bride had to be paid for by the groom, to make up for the loss of her usefulness to her family. The bride's father usually gave her some money called a dowry. The wedding was at the bride's house, and in the evening the groom arrived. In a simple service he took the veil from her face and placed it on his shoulder while the family gave their blessing. The bride and groom then went to their new home, and all their friends who had been invited to the wedding feast waited in the darkness with lamps to light the couple's way (3).

*A Jewish wedding*

## Clothes

Clothes, too, depend on climate and wealth. In Palestine, where it is hot and dry in the day, everyone wore long, flowing robes to keep cool.

The poorer people were known as the fellahin, and they lived in a village with a headman called a sheikh. Their clothes were very simple: for underclothing they wore a loincloth and on top a tunic resembling a dress. A man's tunic came to his knees and was white, but the woman's reached her ankles and was dyed dark blue. She embroidered the front of her dress with traditional patterns learned in her own village.

The man's tunic was fixed at the waist by a girdle, made either of leather or cloth. In it was a pouch or slit to hold money. When a person wanted to move freely, he drew his tunic through his legs and up into his girdle. This was called 'girding up the loins'. His outer garment, or cloak, was made from a piece of heavy woollen cloth with light and dark brown stripes. It was made by wrapping the material round the body, sewing it at the shoulders, and having slits for the arms to go through. It was so important that, by law, it always had to be returned to its owner by night-time.

*Clothes of the poorer people, showing man with loins 'girded'*

## More about Clothes

Many fellahin walked barefoot, but some had simple sandals. The sandal was made of cow-hide and had a long thong attached. This thong was tied round the ankle and the other end was fixed to the sole with a button.

At night-time, the poor loosened their tunic girdles and lay down as they were. They did not possess night-clothes.

Because of the hot sun, the head was always covered. Men wore turbans, but the women wore a head-square folded to make a sunshield for the eyes, and with folds to protect the neck. It was held on by a plaited cord.

The richer person, the belladin, had the same type of clothes, but also wore a short, coloured jacket over the tunic, or better still, a long-sleeved coat. This was made of cotton or even silk, depending on the wealth of the wearer.

Very religious people wore a small leather box strapped to the forehead and left hand. These contained pieces of parchment written with words of their law. They were called phylacteries. Clothes showed the job a person did. Peter wore a 'fisherman's coat', and a teacher or rabbi could be recognised by the blue 'fringe' at the bottom of his coat.

*The various clothes seen in a village street*

# The Farmer's Work

After the autumn rains had softened the soil, the farmer set to work with a wooden plough pulled by an ox. Then as he went up and down the furrows, he scattered the seed by hand from a large open basket.

At reaping time, the corn was either pulled out by hand or cut with a sickle. Early sickles were wooden and set with sharp stones, but later were made of metal. Donkeys took the corn to the threshing floor, and gleaners walked behind the reapers, picking up any stray stalks of corn.

The threshing floor was just hard, level earth. To separate the seeds from the stalks, the corn was spread on the floor and animals walked over it, sometimes pulling a heavy wooden sledge with stones fixed underneath. When the evening breeze came, the farmer 'winnowed' his crop with a five-pronged rake called a 'fan' (4). He pushed the rake into the corn and threw it into the air, the wind carrying the straw and chaff away while the heavier grain fell back to the ground. His wife picked up the straw to use as fuel. That night the farmer slept near his crop to guard it, and next day he measured it into bags ready to sell.

*Farmer winnowing corn, with background of reapers still working in field, and donkey arriving with more corn*

# The Work of the Shepherd
## and the Fisherman

The shepherd's lonely job was to find food for the sheep and protect them from wild animals. In summer, when grass was scarce, he often travelled great distances. At night he checked the sheep into a fold, knowing each one individually. Then he lay across the entrance becoming 'the door of the sheep' (5). Shearing time was at the end of summer, and all who had helped to care for the sheep were invited to the shearing supper. Sheep's wool and goat's hair were used for clothing, and the meat from both animals was valuable. The sheep and goats were never allowed to mix—the goats were driven and the sheep led (6).


A fisherman on Lake Galilee used a rod and line and also a spear, but there were two other main methods of fishing. A circular net was dropped over fishes near the shore, and they were then dragged in. A drag, or seine net was also used: it was of great length, weighted at the bottom and with floats on the top. Sometimes it would be suspended between two boats and the fishes driven ashore, or a circle was formed with the net and it was dragged ashore, with the fish inside. Most fish were sold fresh, but some were salted and sent great distances.

*Shepherd guarding sheep, and fishermen with drag net*

## The Village Craftsmen

The village carpenter made doors, lattice screens to fit the open 'windows', also couches and yokes. He did all the general repair jobs in the village. Because of the dry climate, suitable wood was not very plentiful, and had to be brought from afar.

The villagers did their own spinning and weaving. Goat-hair cloth was made by first taking a bundle of hair, holding it under the arm and twisting it to make a tuft. When the tuft was long enough, a stone was tied to it and gradually spun until it drew out a long, coarse string of goat hair. When woven, the resulting cloth was known as sackcloth, and because it was rough and uncomfortable it was used only for clothes for mourning (7), for nosebags for animals and for tents and curtains. Camel-hair cloth was made in a similar way but was buff in colour instead of black. As well as being comfortable to wear, it was very useful as a second colour when weaving a pattern.

The potter's pots and vases were needed for many purposes such as drinking and storage. The clay was first made ready by mixing to the right consistency with water and being well-trodden by the potter's feet. The potter worked his wheel with his feet while his fingers shaped the clay. When the clay was dry, it was placed in an oven and 'fired'.

*A carpenter and potter at work*

## More about the Craftsmen

The tanner was an important craftsman in New Testament times. Leather, made from the treated skins of sheep and goats, was used for sandals and girdles. It was especially suitable as a cheap material for making containers for liquids, the leather sometimes being cut and sewn into the shape of a bottle.

Military equipment such as helmets, quivers, slings and shields was made of leather, the shields being well oiled to prevent cracking and the penetration of enemy weapons. Leather was seldom used for tents.

Tanning was usually done outside a town and beside a stream. This was because of the unpleasant smell and the need for a plentiful supply of water. The hairs of the skins were removed by smearing with, or soaking in, lime, and the skins were then dried in the sun and treated with oak bark or leaves—and sometimes dyed.

The smith was another important craftsman. Iron-working was discovered about 1200 B.C., but for centuries before that the Palestinians knew how to mine, smelt, refine and work gold, silver and copper. The smiths made a variety of metal vessels and implements— plough-blades, axes, forks, knives and daggers.

*A tanner at work*

## Travel

There were very few good roads in Palestine, and these were mostly built later by the Romans. Stone blocks were laid on a gravel foundation, and sloped so that the water ran away. Milestones marked the distances along raised pavements. Nothing was allowed to block the road in any way; even overhanging trees were cut down.

Other roads were no more than hard earth and could not be used in the wet season. When anyone of importance travelled along such a road, a herald went ahead to tell the villagers to 'make the road straight' (8) by filling in the holes.

Travel was normally on foot, and in groups to stop attacks by robbers. Heavy goods were moved by donkey or ox-cart, though the desert people used camels, and the rich had chariots.

Inns were built for travellers, and they were built round a courtyard where the animals were kept. There were two floors of rooms, which were empty and quite free, but the inn-keeper provided a meal, or anything else needed, for a fee (9). There was another kind of 'inn' which was a rough shelter where the traveller could loosen the burdens on his animal, and then lie down with other persons around a fire. It was this kind of inn in which there was no room for the Holy Family.

*A group of travellers arriving at an inn*

## Towns

When people lived in a fertile part of the country where they could earn more money, they grouped themselves in villages for protection against bands of robbers. If there was a main road near, they were able to trade with the travellers. Possibly the village then grew into a town. If a town was at the junction of two roads it would become very busy indeed. There were only two important towns in the Palestine of the New Testament—Jerusalem, which was the Jewish capital, and Caesarea where the Roman Governor lived.

For protection, a town usually had a wall and a deep ditch around it. The entrance was through a big gateway with a watchtower on the top. Inside the gateway it was cool and shady, so the elders of the town would meet there to talk among themselves and to settle any quarrels that arose among the people.

On the other side of the gateway was an open square where all the merchants jostled one another, trying to sell their wares. Narrow streets ran off from the square, each named after the trade carried on in it. The synagogue was always built in the busiest or highest part of the town so that it could not be missed.

*A town gateway and busy square*

# Jerusalem

Because it was situated at a busy cross-roads, Jerusalem was the most important city in Palestine and had been lived in for three thousand years before New Testament times. But it was still a small city—only four miles right round the walls.

The city was surrounded by hills. To the east was the Mount of Olives which took its name from the trees growing there. On its lower slopes was the Garden of Gethsemane which was separated from Jerusalem by the small river Kidron (10). To the south and west was the Hinnom Valley where the rubbish was burned and the fires never went out. A big moat was dug to cut off the city from the hills in the north, and at one place the shape of the cutting looked something like a skull. It was called Golgotha, which means a skull. It was here that Jesus was crucified.

The city itself was built on two hills, with a valley in between. It was surrounded by thick walls and by the valleys of the Kidron and Hinnom. Jerusalem was very beautiful as it was made of pure white stone, and many of the towers and spires were gilded. From the Mount of Olives, in the setting sun, it looked as if it was made of pure gold.

*View of Jerusalem from Mount of Olives*

## Inside the City

If a traveller went into that part of Jerusalem at the bottom of the Tyropoeon valley, called the Valley of the Cheesemakers, he found himself among the shops where he could buy anything from simple foods to luxurious clothes. This was a very busy area and the sound of bargaining was to be heard everywhere.

To the left, in the west, was the hill where people lived. Here stood the house where Jesus ate the Last Supper. One very imposing house was that belonging to Caiaphas the High Priest. There were many other houses on the hill, always open to visitors because in Jerusalem all beds and meals were free.

At the end of the valley stood the great buildings erected by King Herod—the Theatre where the chariot races were held, the Forum where criminals were tried, and behind them a long viaduct which linked Herod's fine palace on the western hill with the Temple on the eastern. Beyond these buildings lay public gardens and more houses. At the highest point, behind the Temple, was the Castle of Antonia where the Roman troops were stationed. From the castle a lookout could see over the whole city. In front of the Temple, on the traveller's right, were the houses of the priests and the Temple servants.

*View of Jerusalem looking up the Tyropoeon Valley, with small plan of city illustrating the places mentioned*

A. THE HOUSE OF THE LAST SUPPER
B. CASTLE OF ANTONIA
C. HOUSE OF CAIAPHAS
D. TEMPLE AREA
E. HEROD'S PALACE
F. TEMPLE

*VIADUCT*

TYROPOEON VALLEY
(VALLEY OF THE
CHEESEMAKERS)

## The Temple

The Temple was a huge platform built out over the hill, and divided into courtyards by walls. The Temple building itself was in the innermost courtyard called the Court of the Priests. Only the priests were allowed in this courtyard to offer sacrifices or, when it was their turn, to light the lamp or burn the incense in the Temple building (11). Only the High Priest was allowed, once a year into the inner room which was the special meeting place with God.

From a small courtyard, called the Court of Israel, the men were allowed to look in to see the priests at work. Next to it was the Court of Women, where huge offering boxes were kept (12) and where there was a room in which the elders could be questioned (13). Women could go no further.

All this was the Jewish part of the Temple; no Gentiles were allowed in on pain of death. The remainder was called the Court of the Gentiles. Here was the cattle market where sacrificial animals could be bought, and the bankers' tables where ordinary money could be changed into temple money so that the animals could be purchased. The courtyard was surrounded by pillared porches where people could rest and talk. People could walk through from Jerusalem and out of the Golden Gate to the Mount of Olives.

*What Herod's Temple looked like before its destruction*

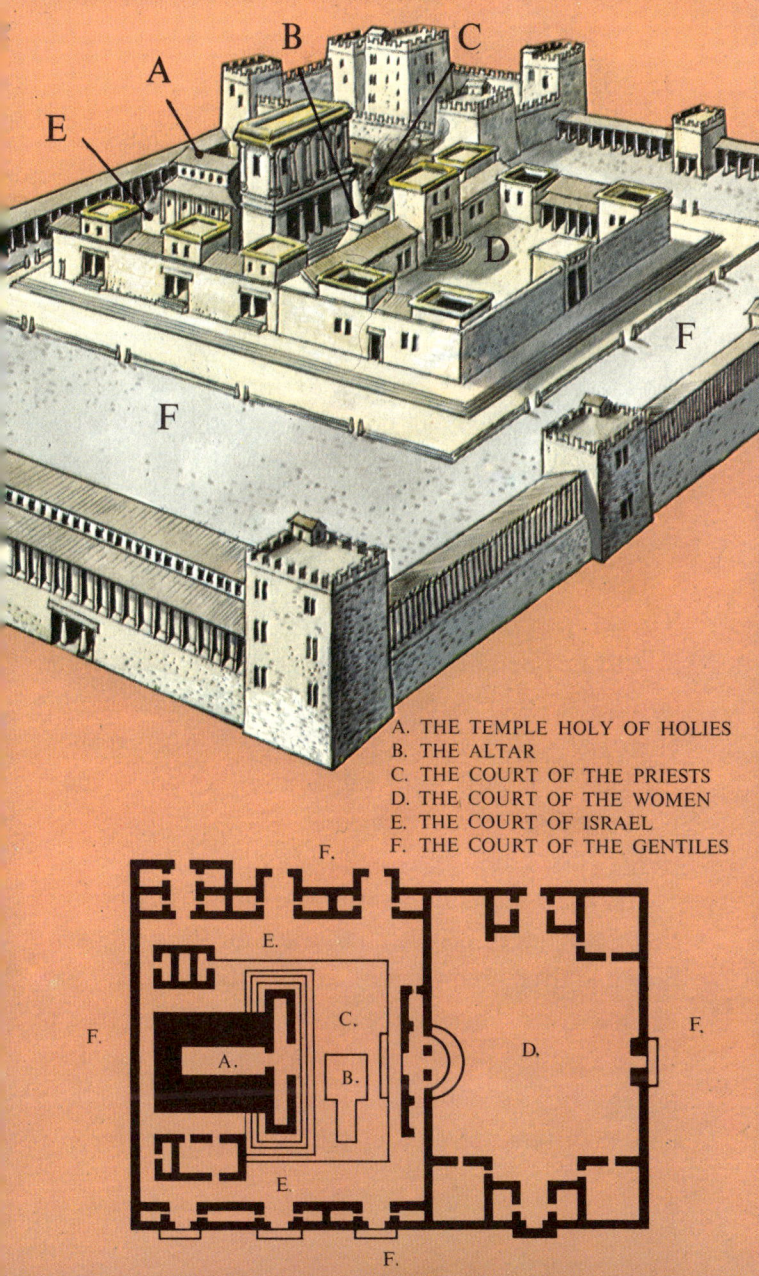

A. THE TEMPLE HOLY OF HOLIES
B. THE ALTAR
C. THE COURT OF THE PRIESTS
D. THE COURT OF THE WOMEN
E. THE COURT OF ISRAEL
F. THE COURT OF THE GENTILES

## The Leaders of the Jews

The Jewish leaders were divided into parties just as people are in our own Parliament. The two main parties were called the Sadducees and the Pharisees. They had their beginnings many years before the New Testament times, when Alexander the Great had conquered Palestine with his Greek army and tried to impose Greek ideas on the Jewish people. Some Jews thought this was a very good idea, but others believed it was the opposite of all God had taught them, and tried to keep themselves free of these ideas.

The Sadducees of the New Testament were the 'Greek' party, and were nearly all related to the priestly families. Like the Greeks they believed that after death, the soul returned to God, and there was no life after death. They did not think God was worried about the kind of life that they led, and so they got as much power and money as they could.

The Pharisees were against these ideas. They believed that God judged people after death for the kind of life they had lived, and so were anxious to keep every part of God's law. Their scribes made laws of their own to try to stop the people from breaking God's law. Ultimately they became more concerned with their own laws than those of God or the needs of other men.

*Scribe at work writing and studying the law*

## The Synagogue

Many years before the time of Jesus, invaders had come to Palestine, destroying the Temple of that time and taking away many Jews as captives to another country. These Jews wanted to worship God and so met together on the Sabbath. The word for 'meeting together' is 'synago' and when they went back to Palestine, the buildings they put up to carry on the worship were called 'synagogues'.

The synagogue was built in the most important position in the town and was always higher than other buildings, either because it was on a hill or because there was a spire on the top.

People went into the synagogue under a porchway where there were two doors. The small one led to a staircase and a gallery. Women and children went in here as they could not take any part in the service.

In the centre of the building was a platform with a big pulpit, containing a reading desk and chairs for the preacher and the ruler of the synagogue. The male worshippers faced the pulpit, and important synagogue members—teachers and readers—faced them from behind it (14). Behind the teachers was a large curtained alcove with a lamp always burning in front. This alcove contained the 'Ark' where the precious Law books were stored. Only Doctors of Law were allowed to open it.

*A synagogue*

## The Synagogue Service

Everyone went quietly into the synagogue, as they were taught that no-one must rush into the House of God. Everyone had to be properly dressed. The men stood before the pulpit and the Ruler of the Synagogue asked the minister to begin the service.

He began by saying two set prayers, and then every-one joined in the Jewish Creed (15). Psalms were sung from the hymn-book, and the Reader left his seat behind the pulpit. First there was a reading from the Scroll of Law (Books of Moses) and later, one from the Prophets. A scroll was a long piece of parchment wound onto two rollers.

The minister sat to give the sermon (16) and after-wards the men in the congregation were allowed to ask him questions. Sometimes an important visiting preacher would be asked to speak instead.

The Ruler of the Synagogue was elected from the village elders and was in charge of all that went on there. He decided on the reader and the preacher. The minister was directly responsible to him.

The synagogue and its services had a great influence on the early Christian churches and those who know the services in the Church of England will see that parts have been taken from the synagogue service.

*Inside of synagogue from Women's Gallery, with service in progress*

## Going to School

The local village school was attached to the synagogue, and it was the minister's job to teach the boys of six or seven years old and upwards.

The Jewish boy never forgot his first day at school. He went at dawn with his father to the synagogue to hear how Moses received the Law. Then he was taken to his teacher's house and welcomed. He was given a slate with passages from the Old Testament written on it. The slate was smeared with honey which he had to lick off (17). He ate small cakes with texts written on them. This was done to show that the purpose of his schooling was that he should absorb the teachings of the Jewish Bible—the Old Testament. This was his only textbook, and as he sat at the feet of his teacher, he learned by repetition.

Every Jewish boy had to learn at home also. From the age of three it was the father's job to teach him the Law and meaning of the Jewish faith, and the many festivals gave good opportunities. His father also had to teach him a trade, as it was a Jewish law that everyone should learn a trade to support himself in time of need. Even the great Apostle Paul was trained to be a tentmaker, though he 'sat at the feet' of the great teacher, Gamaliel (18).

*Jewish boys with their teacher*

## How the Romans came to Palestine

At the time when Jesus was born, the Romans had occupied Palestine for about sixty years. Before this there had been civil war between two powerful brothers, Hyrcanus and Aristobulus and each wanted to be the High Priest and rule the country. South of Palestine was another country called Edom, and its king—named Antipater—helped one of the brothers and then asked for additional help from the Roman army. The Romans came—but they would not go away! They made Palestine part of the Roman Empire and let Antipater rule the country for them. His son's name was Herod the Great, about whom we read in the story of the birth of Jesus.

Herod ruled over the whole country and was a cruel and evil man. He murdered many of his sons, and even his wife, the beautiful Jewish princess Mariamme. Even the Roman Emperor said he would sooner be Herod's pig than his son.

When Herod died, Palestine was divided between his remaining sons. The most important was Herod Antipas who ruled in Galilee and Peraea and who beheaded John the Baptist (19). Another son, called Archelaeus (20) who ruled over Samaria, Judaea and Edom, was so bad that the Romans replaced him by their own governor called a procurator. Pontius Pilate was procurator at the time of Jesus' death.

*The cruel Herod the Great*

## Roman Government

There were some good results of Roman rule in Palestine. Excellent roads were made, and a fine harbour built at Caesarea where the procurator lived. Public buildings were put up and law and order kept by the soldiers. As a result there was increased trading and wealth.

But there were many things that made the Jews unhappy. A Jew could be forced to carry a soldier's pack for one mile (21). Sacrifices had to be made each day in the Temple for the Roman Emperor, with a prayer that God would help him. The High Priest was under the control of the procurator. Annas, the High Priest, had been deposed and Caiaphas put in his place, but both were recognised by the Jews (22). Those people who hated the Romans enough to try and get rid of them were called Zealots.

Taxes had to be paid too—a fifth of a person's income each year. They were collected by publicans (23) who were also Jews, and who were looked upon as traitors by their countrymen.

Latin was the official language of the Empire, but most people in the East spoke Greek. The New Testament was written in Greek. Most people in Palestine spoke in Aramaic, and a few of Christ's Aramaic words are preserved for us in the Bible (24).

*Publican at work on quayside of Caesarea with Roman soldier standing guard*

## Keeping the Peace

The Romans allowed the Jews to punish people who had done wrong, as long as the crime was not too great. Quarrels in the town or village were settled by the elders who sat in the gate. Any religious matters were dealt with by officials at the local synagogue (25).

The most important court the Jews had was the Sanhedrin, made up of the High Priest and seventy Pharisees and Sadducees. They met in the Hall of Hewn Stones in the Temple. This court was very powerful (26) but could not pass the death sentence. Permission for this had to come from the procurator. Procurators tried any crimes against the Roman Empire.

The Romans had to keep the peace between the Jews and Samaritans, who hated one another because of a quarrel which had started in Old Testament times. Years before, the Jews in the north lost their leaders during an invasion, but accepted foreigners who came to replace the leaders. The Jews in the south felt that this made their northern neighbours impure and therefore would accept no help from them in repairing the Jerusalem Temple. The northern people, calling themselves Samaritans, built a temple of their own, only to have it burned down by a southern army shortly before the Romans came.

*Jesus standing before Pontius Pilate*

## Money Matters

In the years before the New Testament times, many Jews were taken from their homes by different invaders. They were never allowed to return to Palestine and instead settled and made a living in the country to which they had been taken. This movement was called the 'Dispersion'.

Starting a living in another city was no easy task, as crafts were usually controlled by Craft Guilds, which were similar in many ways to the Trades Union Movement. The Guilds tried to shut out the Jews, and there was no opportunity for public service. They could only make a living by trading, which they did very well, and by lending to other people, at a high rate of interest, the profits from trading. As a result, many became very wealthy, though this was frowned upon by the Jewish leaders who were aware of the strict laws in the Old Testament against lending money for interest.

The money system used in New Testament times was very complicated. There was an international Roman coinage, but at the same time local states within the Empire could issue their own coins which were legal in that state. The mite in the New Testament was a local Jewish copper coin of small value, but the penny was the Roman silver denarius, which was a day's wage for a labourer.

*Jews trading*

Series 649
A Ladybird Book